The hollyhock's bright blooms are arranged in tall spires.

5

At that time, ferns and other primitive plants covered the earth. But over millions of years, flowering plants have edged out the others. There are now some 240 million different kinds of flowering plants, growing on every continent except Antarctica.

The flowering plant family includes some members that may surprise you. Grasses are flowering plants, although most people don't think of them as such. So are many trees, including oaks and maples. Their flowers are not as flashy or colorful as those of garden plants. Without its flowers, an oak tree could not make acorns, its seeds. And without acorns, new oak trees couldn't grow.

Flowers come in all colors, shapes, and sizes. The world's smallest flower belongs to duck-

The flowers of grass are small, so most people don't notice them.

6

weed, a water plant that floats on the surface of ponds. Duckweed flowers are as small as $\frac{1}{16}$ inch (1.6 millimeters) long. The largest flower belongs to a rafflesia, a rare plant from the rain forests of Sumatra and Borneo. This plant has no leaves or stems of its own. Instead, it is a parasite that grows within the woody stem of a tropical vine. When the plant blooms, a huge orange bud breaks through the bark of the vine stem. The bud opens into a flower that may measure as much as 3 feet (0.9 meters) across and weigh more than 15 pounds (6.8 kilograms).

Oak trees have two kinds of flowers: male (right) and female (below).

A spring garden features flowers of many different kinds.

PARTS OF A FLOWER

Large or small, flowers begin as tightly closed buds. **Sepals**, which often look like small leaves, cover a flower bud and protect it. The bud swells as the structures inside grow. Finally, it bursts open, and the sepals are pushed aside by the petals. The petals are the largest and most colorful parts of most flowers, but this isn't always so.

As this black-eyed Susan flower opens, the green sepals are pushed back by the yellow petals.

The fucshia is a "perfect" flower. It has both male and female parts.

In the center of a flower, surrounded by the petals, are the important reproductive parts. The flowers of many plants have both male and female parts. They are called **perfect flowers**. Other plants have separate male and female flowers. Oak trees and the pussy willows are examples of plants with these **imperfect flowers**.

Stamens are the male structures. Most flowers have several stamens. Each has two parts—a thin stalk, called a **filament**, with an **anther** on top. The anthers are filled with tiny **pollen** grains, which contain sperm—male reproductive cells.

Pistils are the female structures. Most flowers have one pistil. It, too, has several parts. At the base of the pistil is the **ovary**. Inside the ovary are tiny compartments called **ovules**, which contain eggs—female reproductive cells. Above the ovary is a stalk, called a **style**, topped by a sticky pad, the **stigma**.

The pussy willow has "imperfect" flowers, with either male or female parts. These are male flowers.

11

The stargazer lily clearly shows the female pistil surrounded by male stamens.

Inset: The sunflower is really a tightly packed cluster of many tiny flowers.

stigma

anther

style

filament

petals

ovary

These structures are easy to see in some flowers, such as the lily. They are harder to spot in others. Take a close look at a daisy or a sunflower, for example. What seems to be a single flower is really a tightly packed cluster of many tiny flowers, called florets. The florets that fill the center are shaped like tiny tubes. These are disk florets. Those around the edge each have a single large petal. They're called ray florets, because their petals stick out like rays around the center.

For seeds to form, pollen must get from the anthers, at the tips of the stamens, to the stigma, at the top of the pistil.

13

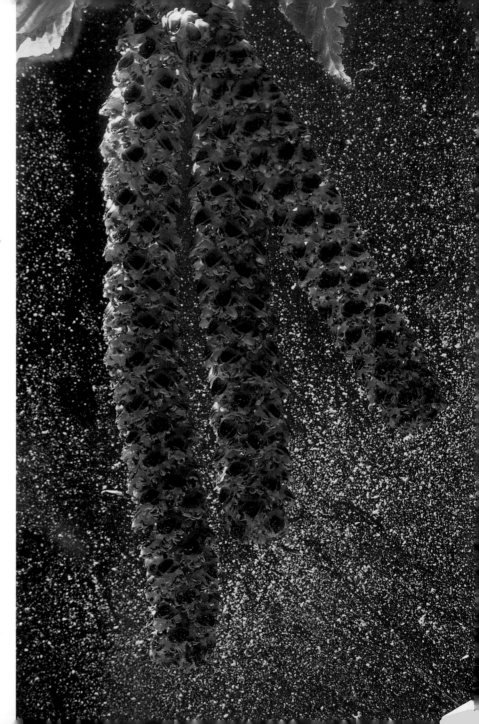

POLLEN ON THE MOVE

For seeds to form, pollen must get from the anther to the pistil. Flowers are designed to make that happen, and they do it in various ways. Pollen may fall to the pistil from an anther on the same flower. This is called **self-pollination**. Often, though, pollen comes from another plant of the same type. **Cross-pollination**, as this is called, mixes **genes** from different parent plants. When seeds form, they carry traits from both plants. This helps produce healthy, strong new plants.

Wind may carry pollen from one plant to another. Many trees and grasses rely on the wind for pollination. They make lots of pollen and release it in clouds. This works for the plants, but it's misery for people who are allergic to plant pollens!

Like many trees, the white birch spreads its pollen on the wind.

FOUL-SMELLING FLORA

Bees and butterflies flock to flowers with sweet fragrances. But not all flowers smell so nice. Some flowers smell like rotting meat! Carrion flowers, as they're called, attract beetles and flies that feed and sometimes lay their eggs on carrion and wastes. To them, the stench of rotting meat is as sweet as honey. The flowers fool the insects. As they crawl around looking for the food they think is there, they pollinate the flowers so that seeds can form.

One of these plant stinkers is the rafflesia, which produces the largest flower in the world. Its common name is "stinking corpse lily." Another is the eastern skunk cabbage, which is common in swampy areas of eastern North America. The skunk cabbage has tiny male and female flowers packed tightly around a sort of column called a spadix. You probably wouldn't notice them—but you can't miss their stench.

A bumblebee probes a dandelion with its tongue, seeking nectar.

Many plants rely on pollinators—insects such as bees and butterflies, birds such as hummingbirds, and even bats and other animals. The scents and bright colors of flowers attract these pollinators. Especially bright flowers are sending the "loudest" message to the pollinators, hoping to entice them into transferring pollen from one plant to another. Many insects see colors differently than people do. They can detect ultraviolet light, which people can't see. To a bee, a flower may seem even more vivid than it does to you.

15

This wrinkled rose flower will fade as seeds begin to form.

FROM FLOWER TO SEED

The pistil's sticky tip is a pollen trap. When a grain of pollen lands on it, the pollen sticks fast. The pollen grain swells, and soon it grows a thin tube that reaches down through the style to an ovule. Two sperm cells travel down the pollen tube. When they reach the ovule, a seed begins to form.

One sperm cell joins with an egg cell. The egg cell begins to divide to form a plant **embryo**, which will develop into a new plant. The second sperm cell joins with another cell in the ovule, called the central cell. This cell begins to divide to form the **endosperm**, the part of the seed where food is stored for the growing embryo. The ovule itself forms the outer wall of the seed.

A cutaway view of a wrinkled rose ovary shows the seeds forming inside.

Bean pods are the fruit of bean plants. They protect the seeds.

Animals such as gray squirrels help spread the seeds of apple trees and other plants.

The flower's job is done. As seeds form, the flower petals and other structures wither and drop away. The ovary remains, growing larger as the seeds develop inside. It will form the plant's fruit. A fruit may be fleshy, like an apple. It may be hard-shelled, like an acorn. Or it may be a dry pod, like a bean pod. Whatever the type, the fruit's main purpose is to protect the seeds.

When the seeds are ready, the plant releases them. Different plants spread their seeds in different ways—on the wind, in water, or with the help of birds and other animals. When a seed lands in the right spot, and if conditions are right, it will sprout. In time, the new plant will produce flowers and seeds of its own.

SURVIVAL STRATEGIES

Flowering plants need light, warmth, and moisture to grow and bloom. In tropical areas, plants can flower all year. But where winters are cold, conditions are too harsh. Plants in these climates have developed several ways to survive when they are not flowering.

White daisies and yellow marigolds make a colorful garden border.

PETAL POWER

Scientists divide flowering plants into two groups, based on structures in their seeds. The structures are seed leaves, or cotyledons, which help provide food for the tiny new plant inside. Plants with one cotyledon are monocots, and plants with two cotyledons are dicots.

You don't need a seed to tell a monocot from a dicot, though. One way to tell which plants belong in which group is by counting the petals in their flowers. Most monocots have petals in multiples of three. Trillium and lilies are examples. Most dicots, including roses and many other flowers, have petals in multiples of four or five.

The trillium, with petals in multiples of three, is a monocot.

Some flowering plants grow, bloom, and make seeds all in a single season. The plants die at the end of the season, but their seeds will sprout the next year. These plants are called **annuals**. They include popular garden flowers such as pansies, marigolds, zinnias, and petunias, as well as common vegetables such as beans, tomatoes, and corn.

Other plants take two years to grow and produce seeds. In the first year, the plant develops roots and a low crown of leaves. It spends the winter in a dormant (inactive) state. During the second year, it produces its flowers and seeds, and then dies. These plants are **biennials**. They include garden flowers such as foxgloves.

Annuals such as the pansy grow, bloom, and make seeds in one year.

Dame's rocket is a perennial. It blooms for many years.

Perennials live for many years. They may bloom and produce seeds every year or less often. Some, such as peonies and other garden plants, die back to the ground in fall. But their roots survive and send up new shoots in spring. Many flowering trees and shrubs, such as most roses, shed their leaves in fall and grow new leaves the next spring.

Foxglove is a biennial. It takes two years to bloom and produce seeds.

23

People plant flower gardens to enjoy their natural beauty.

FLOWERS AND PEOPLE

People have always valued flowers most for their beauty. But people have found many uses for flowers, too. The flowers of some plants are used in herbal teas and folk remedies. Some flowers are key ingredients in important medicines. Foxglove, for example, is used to make digitalis, which is a valuable medication for heart patients. Medicines made from rosy periwinkle are used to treat Hodgkin's disease and childhood leukemia. Many of these (and other) flowers are not edible—foxglove is highly poisonous—but some, such as certain violets or nasturtiums, may wind up in salads or other dishes. Certain fragrant flowers are processed to extract oils used in perfumes.

Flowers have also given rise to many folktales and traditional beliefs. In Asia, for example chrysanthemums are symbols of long life, purity, and perfection. The Order of the Chrysanthemum is the highest honor a person can receive in Japan.

Roses are among the flowers used to make perfume.

Flowers play a very important role in the web of life. Earth's great variety of flowering plants supports a great variety of animals—including people. From apples and beets to yams and zucchini, nearly all the fruits, vegetables, and grains that people eat come from flowering plants. In a very real way, people depend on flowers.

Flowering plants are important to the survival of many animals, including this curious raccoon.

TALES OF TULIPS

In Holland in the 1600s, some tulip bulbs began to produce flowers with streaks and varied colors. A plant virus caused the changes, but no one knew that. Because these bulbs were so rare, they were in great demand. People paid huge prices for them, figuring that seeds from the flowers could be grown to produce more streaked tulips. Some people invested all their money in tulip bulbs. Then the tulip bubble burst, and fortunes were lost. But the Dutch went on to develop a thriving flower-growing industry. Today their tulips are admired—especially the streaky ones.

Fortunes were made—and lost—in the Dutch tulip trade.

2

🌼 🌼 🌼

Growing and Collecting Flowers

Flowers are great for close-up study because they're easy to find. Even in winter, there are probably flowers at your local market. In summer, gardens are full of flowers. Wildflowers grow along roads, in fields, and even in vacant lots.

If you want to pick flowers from a garden, be sure to ask the gardener's permission first. Wildflowers may seem to be there for the taking, but many kinds of wildflowers are rare or endangered. They are also part of the natural beauty in an environment—and we should all make sure we disturb nature as little as possible.

There are many kinds of flowers that can be grown from seeds.

29

Flowering plants such as petunias are sold at garden centers.

Unless you know that a particular flower isn't rare, it's best to leave wildflowers where they grow. That way, the plants can form seeds and reproduce.

The best flowers to pick are those you grow yourself. Many kinds of flowers are easy to grow. If you don't have space for a garden, you can plant a flower box. This chapter will tell you how to do that, and how to press and save flowers.

GROWING FLOWERS

You can buy young flowering plants at a garden center or grow your own plants from seeds. If you decide to grow your own, choose kinds that are easy to start from seeds. We used marigolds. Zinnias, sunflowers, and nasturtiums are also good choices.

STARTING SEEDS

Most flowering plants grow best if they're started in small pots before planting in the garden. (Sunflowers are an exception. They don't like to be moved, so it's best to plant them where they can grow to full size.)

What to Do:

1. To make pots, punch holes in the bottom of the containers. This will let extra water drain out. (Instead of milk cartons, you can use disposable drinking cups, plant trays, small flowerpots, or peat pots from a garden center.)
2. Fill the containers with potting soil. Write the name of the flower on a Popsicle stick using a pencil or waterproof ink. Push the stake into the potting soil so you'll remember what's planted there.

3. Place two seeds in the soil. Seeds don't always sprout, so by planting two you improve your chances of getting a plant to grow. Different kinds of seeds must be planted at different depths, so follow the planting directions on the seed package.

4. Sprinkle the seeds and soil with water until evenly moist.

5. Set the pots on a tray, to catch any water that leaks through. Keep them indoors in a warm, sunny place. Keep the soil moist by spraying or sprinkling with water whenever it begins to dry out.

6. If both seeds in a pot sprout, remove the smaller one by pinching it off with your fingers, right at soil level. This will give the other plant room to grow.

7. When your plants have their second set of true leaves, you can move them to the garden or a flower box.

What You Need:

* Flower box
* Gravel
* Potting soil
* Plant food or compost
* Flowering plants

PLANTING A FLOWER BOX

What to Do:

1. You can buy a flower box at a garden center. Choose one with holes in the bottom so that water will drain out. Put a layer of gravel or small stones in the bottom of the box to help moisture drain away from the plant roots.

2. Mix some of the plant food or compost with your potting soil. Add this mixture to the flower box. Make a hole in the mix for the roots of each plant.

3. Hold each plant upside down and carefully shake it from its container. Be careful not to damage the roots. Place the root clump in the hole. Cover the roots with soil.

4. When all the plants are in the box, water the soil thoroughly. Put the box in a place that has the right amount of light for your flowers. (The seed packets have this information.) Water the plants whenever the soil starts to dry out.

33

PRESSING FLOWERS

Flowers fade, but you can save some by pressing them. Pansies, nasturtiums, and other small, simple flowers press more easily than big flowers or those with lots of petals, such as zinnias. Here is a simple method:

- Place a clean sheet of paper in a large heavy book. Then lay the flowers on the paper.
- Place a paper towel over the flowers, and then carefully close the book.
- Stack more books on top of the first book. Your flowers will be dry in about a month.

3

Investigating Flowers

How much light do flowers need to bloom? Can you make cut flowers last by putting pennies in the water? How do anthers affect the life of flowers? In this chapter you'll find some activities and experiments that will help you answer these and other questions. Many of the activities use houseplants or cut flowers, so they can be done year-round.

WHAT KIND OF LIGHT DO AFRICAN VIOLETS PREFER?

African violets are popular flowering houseplants. Like other plants, they must have the right conditions to bloom well. That includes the right kind of light. Will African violets bloom best in direct sunlight or in bright but indirect light? Decide what you think, and then do this experiment to find out.

What You Need:
* Two African violet plants, similar in size and number of flowers, in two identical pots

What to Do:

1. Put one plant in a south-facing window or another place where it will get direct sunlight. Put the second plant in a north-facing window or another place where it will get bright but indirect light.
2. Keep the soil in both pots evenly moist, so that the main difference in growing conditions is the amount of light the plants get. You may find that the pot in direct sunlight dries out faster and needs water more often than the second pot.
3. Over several weeks, observe the flowers and condition of the leaves on both plants. Keep notes on your observations.

Results: Compare the two plants to see which has healthier leaves and more flowers.

Conclusion: What do your results tell you about the type of light that African violets like best? Repeat this experiment with other plants, such as geraniums, and different light conditions. How do the results differ?

What You Need:

* Any of these items: Pennies, vinegar, lemon juice, carbonated water, sugar, aspirin, packaged flower preservative
* Cut flowers, all the same kind and at the same stage of bloom
* Containers for the flowers, all the same size
* Labels

WHAT HELPS CUT FLOWERS LAST?

Everyone wants cut flowers to last as long as possible. People have tried all sorts of ways. Some people toss pennies in the water. Others add aspirin, vinegar, sugar, or other substances. Some pinch off the flowers' anthers, which hold pollen. Do any of these methods work? Make a prediction, based on what you know about flowers. Here are two experiments that will help you find out if your prediction is right.

WILL ADDING ITEMS TO WATER HELP CUT FLOWERS LAST?

What to Do:

1. Place an equal amount of water in each container.
2. Keep plain water in one container. Add a different item to each of the others. For example, put several pennies in one, an aspirin in another, a spoonful of sugar in a third, and equal amounts of lemon juice and packaged preservative (from a flower shop) in the others.
3. Cut the flower stems so they're all the same length. Cut off the lower leaves, so leaves won't be in the water.
4. Place some flowers in each container. Check them each day to see how well they're lasting. Keep notes of your observations.

Results: Note how long the flowers in each container last. Which lasted longest?

Conclusion: Did any of the additives help the flowers? You can repeat the experiment using combinations of some of the materials—for example, lemon juice and sugar.

WILL REMOVING ANTHERS HELP OR HARM CUT FLOWERS?

What to Do:

1. For this experiment, select flowers that are just beginning to open. Lilies work well because the anthers are large and easy to see.
2. Locate the stamens. They're usually thin stalks clustered around in the center of the flower.
3. On half the flowers, pinch off all the anthers, the pollen-making parts at the tips of the stamens. Leave the other flowers whole.
4. Cut the flower stems so they're all the same length. Place them in equal-sized containers with equal amounts of water.

Results: Note how long the flowers in each container last.

Conclusion: Did removing the anthers help or harm the flowers? Can you think of reasons why?

DO FLOWER BUDS NEED LIGHT TO OPEN?

Light is very important for the plants as they are growing. But how does light affect a plant's flowers? Will buds open as quickly in darkness as in light? Decide what you think, and then do this experiment to find out.

What to Do:

1. Find a plant or plants with several flower buds at about the same stage of development. For best results, choose a plant that has small flowers and isn't in direct sunlight.

2. Cut a piece of black construction paper and tape or staple it into a cone shape. The cone should be small enough to fit inside a plastic sandwich bag, but large enough at the narrow end to slip over a flower bud.

3. Put the cone over a bud. Then cut a piece of black cloth to cover the opening at the end of the cone. Push the cloth into the opening, overlapping if necessary to keep light from reaching the bud inside.

41

4. Put a sandwich bag over the cone. Use string or a rubber band to tie it loosely to the flower stem.

5. Place sandwich bags without black cones over another bud that's at about the same stage of development as the first bud. Tie it loosely the same way.

6. If the stems flop, prop them up using a sturdy stick and a clothespin. Check the buds in the bags every day.

Results: Watch to see if the buds open together or if one opens faster.

Conclusion: Did blocking out light affect the buds? Try this experiment with different kinds of flowers, and see if your results are the same.

MORE FLOWER ACTIVITIES

1. Go on a flower hunt. How many different kinds of flowers can you find? Identify the different kinds, using a wildflower or garden guide. Then make a flower chart. For each type, show the number of flowers on a stem, the size of the flowers, the height of the stem, the scent, the colors, and the number of petals, stamens, and stigmas. How many **dicots** did you collect? How many **monocots**?

2. Get the buzz on bees by watching as they visit flowers. Can you see the bee's long tongue probing into the flower? Is there pollen on the bee's leg or body? Where?

3. Try your hand at plant breeding. You'll need a garden and patience for this—it takes time. Begin by cross-pollinating some flowers. Pumpkins work well, but you could use other plants. Here's what to do:

   • Pumpkins have separate male and female flowers (see the photos). As soon as a female flower opens, gently take off the petals and cover the remaining flower with a plastic bag.

   • Use a small brush to collect some pollen from a male flower. If you can, get pollen from a different variety of pumpkin.

   • Brush the pollen on the pistil top, and then recover the pistil.

   • A pumpkin should grow from the cross-pollinated pistil. Save the seeds from that pumpkin. Plant them, and enjoy the results of your plant breeding. If you crossed two kinds of pumpkins, see how the new pumpkins are like or unlike their parents.

Top: Male pumpkin flower.
Above: Female pumpkin flower. *43*

RESULTS AND CONCLUSIONS

Here are some possible results and conclusions for the activities on pages 37 to 42. Because many conditions affect the way flowering plants grow, you may not get the same results. If your outcomes differ, try to think of reasons why. What do you think led to your results? Repeat the activity, and see if the outcome is the same.

What kind of light do African violets prefer?

African violets usually grow best in indirect light. But other kinds of plants have different needs for light. Geraniums, for example, do well in full sunlight.

Will adding items to water help cut flowers last?

You may find that most items added to the water don't make a big difference. Sugar may help the flowers last a bit longer because it feeds them. Lemon juice and vinegar make the water more acid, and that may also help the flowers last. The best results come from using packaged additives that are specially prepared for preserving cut flowers. These additives contain sugar and an acidifier as well as antibacterial chemicals. The antibacterial chemicals help keep bacteria from growing in the water and decaying the flower stems.

Will removing anthers help or harm cut flowers?

The flowers with anthers removed usually last longer. The reason is that energy that would have been used to develop pollen in the anthers goes to help all the other parts instead. This is a technique that flower shops often use, as it doesn't change the appearance of the flowers too much.

Do flower buds need light to open?

You may find that both buds open at about the same time. Although plants need light to grow and make flowers, the flowers themselves are not usually affected by light. Some flowers open each day and close again each night. These types may open more slowly inside the dark bag.

SOME WORDS ABOUT FLOWERS

annuals Flowering plants that grow, flower, and make seeds in one year.

anther The pollen-making structure on top of a stamen.

biennials Flowering plants that take two years to grow and produce seeds.

cotyledons Seed leaves, which help provide food for the tiny new plant inside a seed.

cross-pollination Transfer of pollen from one plant to the ovary of another.

dicots Plants with two cotyledons.

embryo The part of a seed that will form a new plant.

endosperm The part of a seed where food is stored.

filament The thin stalk of a stamen.

genes Materials inside cells that determine the traits of living things.

imperfect flowers Flowers with only male or only female parts.

monocots Plants with one cotyledon.

ovary The base of the pistil, containing the ovules.

ovules Compartments in the ovary that hold female sex cells (eggs).

perennials Flowering plants that live for many years.

perfect flowers Flowers with both male and female parts.

pistil The female part of a flower.

pollen A fine powder that contains a plant's male sex cells (sperm).

self-pollination Transfer of a plant's pollen to its own ovules.

sepals Leaflike flower parts that cover and protect the flower bud.

stamens The male structures in a flower.

stigma A sticky pad on top of the pistil, designed to trap pollen.

style The long neck of the pistil.

45

FOR MORE INFORMATION

Books

Burns, Diane L. *Wildflowers, Blooms, and Blossoms.* NorthWord Press, 1998.

Burton, Jane, and Kim Taylor. *The Nature and Science of Flowers.* Gareth Stevens, 1998.

Goodman, Susan E. *Seeds, Stems, and Stamens: The Ways Plants Fit into Their World.* Millbrook Press, 2001

Hood, Susan. *Wildflowers (National Audubon Society First Field Guide).* Scholastic Trade, 1998.

Howell, Laura, et. al. *World of Plants (Library of Science).* Usborne, 2002.

Maurer, Tracy Nelson. *Growing Flowers.* Rourke, 2001.

WEB SITES:

KinderGarden
Find fun garden activities and more.
http://aggie-horticulture.tamu.edu/kindergarden/index.html

Wildflowers in Bloom
Learn about some of America's showiest wildflowers.
http://aggie-horticulture.tamu.edu/wildseed/ wildflowers.html

SOURCES FOR SEEDS

You can buy flower seeds at garden centers and hardware and home supply stores. Check to be sure that the seeds have not been treated with fungicides or other chemicals. You can also order untreated seeds through the mail. These companies provide catalogs:

Burpee Seeds
300 Park Avenue
Warminster, PA 18991
800-888-1447
www.burpee.com

Johnny's Selected Seeds
184 Foss Hill Road
Albion, ME 04910
207-437-9294
www.johnnyseeds.com

Park Seed Co.
1 Parkton Avenue
Greenwood, SC 29647-0001
www.parkseed.com

Shepherd's Garden Seeds
30 Irene Street
Torrington, CT 06790-6658
800-503-9624
www.shepherdseeds.com

Territorial Seed Company
P.O. Box 157
Cottage Grove, OR 97424-0061
www.territorial-seed.com

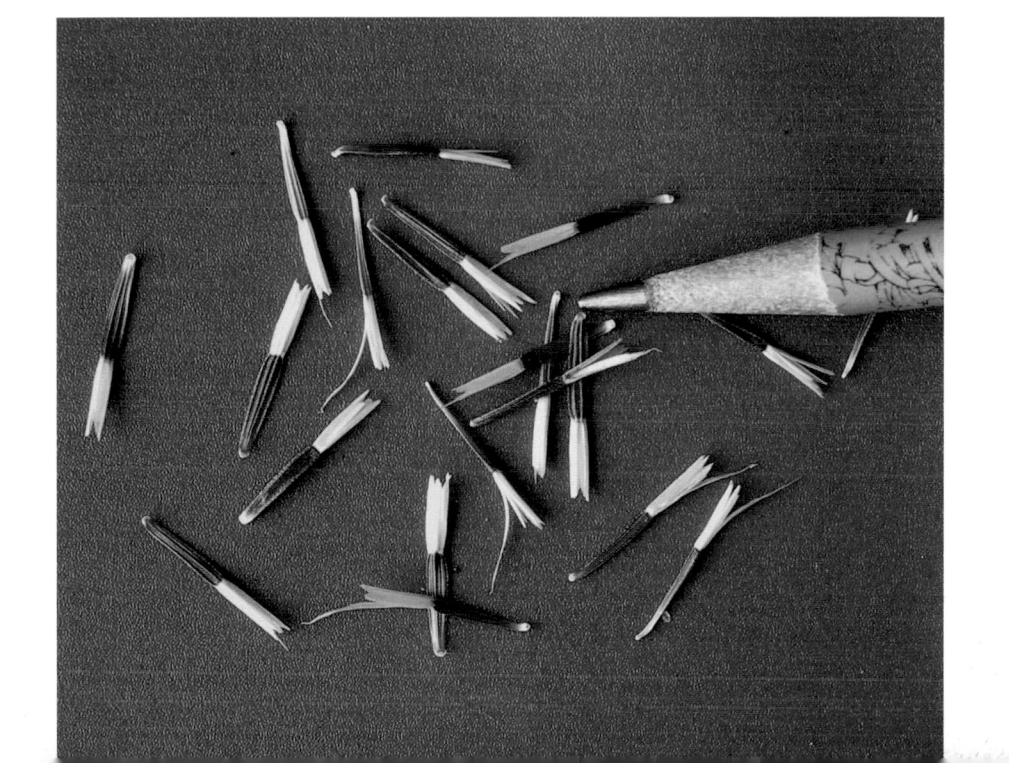

INDEX

Activities, 43
African violets, 37, 44
Age of dinosaurs, 4–6
Annuals, 22
Antarctica, 6

Biennials, 22
Buds, 9, 41, 44

Carrion flowers, 15
Cotyledons, 21
Cut flowers, 38–40, 44

Duckweed, 6-7

Embryo, 17

Florets, 13
Fruit, 19, 26

Grasses, 6, 14
Growing flowers, 28–33

Herbal tea, 25
Hodgkin's disease, 25

Medicines, 25

Oak tree, 6, 11
Order of the Chrysanthemum, the, 25

Perennials, 23
Perfect flowers, 11
Perfume, 25
Petals, 9, 11, 13, 19, 21, 34
Pistils, 11, 14, 17, 43
Pollen, 14–15, 17, 43
Pollinators, 15
Pressing, 34

Rafflesia, 7, 15

Sepals, 9
Stamens, 11, 43

Tulips, 27

Ultraviolet light, 15

Wildflowers, 28
Wind, 14, 19